Copyright © 2015 by Victor Joseph. 621822

ISBN: Softcover   978-1-5035-2267-1
       Hardcover   978-1-5035-2266-4
       EBook   978-1-5035-2268-8

All rights reserved. No part of this book may be reproduced or transmitted in any form or by any means, electronic or mechanical, including photocopying, recording, or by any information storage and retrieval system, without permission in writing from the copyright owner.

Rev. date: 10/05/2015

To order additional copies of this book, contact:
Xlibris
1-888-795-4274
www.Xlibris.com
Orders@Xlibris.com

Danes are Great!
Follow the adventures of Brando & Kruger

The Sleepover & It's Snowing

by
Victor Joseph
Illustrated By: Martha Rast

To all dogs everywhere,
and those who care for them.

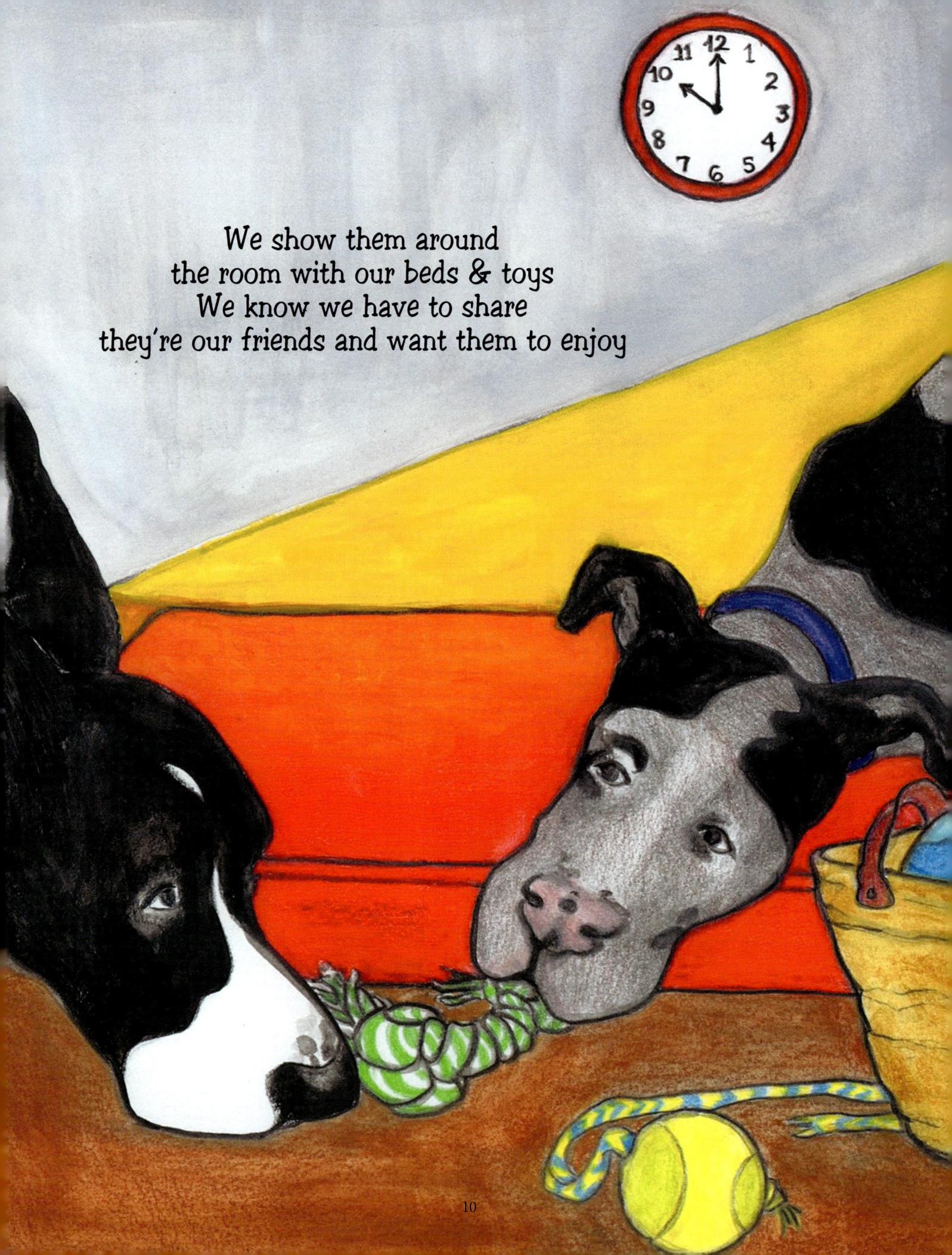

We show them around
the room with our beds & toys
We know we have to share
they're our friends and want them to enjoy

Each of us picks a toy
and are ready to go outside
Joseph opens the door
heading towards the trees where
we like to run and hide

Afterwards, it's off to our room
with one last chance to play
Good thing Luna & Neo sleepover
for its been one long fun day!

It's Snowing

"Brando! Kruger!
Holdup for me!
Don't go too fast
be careful of the trees!"

Joseph tells us
so that we can be safe
He doesn't want us to get hurt
but it's hard for us to wait

We love when it snows
it makes for such fun
It can last a long time
even when the sky is
clear & full of sun

The trails are covered
but we know are way around
No bike for Joseph
so he keeps up, following the
crunching snow sound

Hello! I'm Victor, here with Brando & Kruger, at the beach in Long Island, NY, one of our favorite places for adventure! Whatever the season, the beach is a great place to explore and get some exercise in.

This is the third book in the Danes are Great! series and it contains two stories, The Sleepover & It's Snowing.

Our adventures over the years, along with my desire for quality parent/child time and the need for children to enjoy reading early on, drove me to write the Danes are Great! book series.

So come along with Brando & Kruger on adventures that will enliven your imagination whilst learning some fundamental reading skills.

Perhaps you'll conjure up a story of your own.

Enjoy!

Martha Rast

Martha Rast was born and raised in Minneapolis, MN. She attended both The School of the Art Institute of Chicago, and the Minneapolis College of Art and Design, where she studied for her B.F.A. in Painting and Drawing, and her Professional Certificate in Art Education. She is inspired by her children and the wonder of nature around her.

Martha's first illustrated book Mitzvah the Mutt received the following awards:

¤ Sydney Taylor Notable Book for Older Readers

¤ 2010 Bronze Medalist in Moonbeam Children's Book Award for Juvenile Fiction

Written by Sylvia Rouss for Yotzeret Publishing.

Her first book by author Victor Joseph is called, "Danes Are Great! Follow the Adventures of Brando and Kruger" by Xlibris Publishing. She is thrilled to bring you these next two adventures of these adorable dogs.

Edwards Brothers Malloy
Thorofare, NJ USA
September 30, 2016